Sparky's Mama

by Sandy Stream
Illustrated by Yoko Matsuoka

Sparky's Mama. By Sandy Stream
Illustrated by Yoko Matsuoka
Edited by Tomoko Matsuoka

ISBN: 978-0-9739481-3-4

Copyright © 2014 by Sandy Stream Publishing. Montreal, Canada.
All rights reserved. No part of this book may be reproduced, stored in a retrieval system, or transmitted in any form or by any means without the written permission of Sandy Stream Publishing.

On a Personal Note

Einstein said, "Life is like riding a bicycle. To keep your balance, you must keep moving."

So what happens to our balance and to our bodies when we are unable to move despite having a tremendously strong impulse to do so? The illustrations in this book are meant to show you what we often feel, but do not see.

We are often so busy in our thoughts that we cannot see what happens to our bodies when we are frozen. Through yoga, meditation, or with the help of a therapist or healer, we can learn to observe ourselves honestly, and it is with this honesty that we can see where time is standing still.

Seeing the effect of this inability to move is the first and very difficult step one must take toward healing. However, it is still just the first step. In the next book, we can see what must be done next to complete the natural healing cycle.

Sandy Stream

Based on *many* true stories

Once upon a time there was a mama bird that made a nest and laid three eggs.

Everyone called her River because she flew as if she were dancing fluidly and naturally— like a river.

River lived in a beautiful world. It had rainbows and sunshine and beautiful trees. But it also had big giants who did whatever they wanted.

River had seen many giants do whatever they wanted with small animals. She was careful to build her nest away from anywhere she had ever seen a giant.

When her first egg hatched, she named her baby bird Sparky because he had a lovely sparkle in his eyes.

When her second baby bird was born, she called him Feathers because he was as light as a feather.

When her third baby bird was born, she called him Flex because he was so flexible when he crawled out of the little hole in his shell.

One terrible evening, a giant came and snatched Sparky from River's arms. River was frantic. Her heart was beating very fast.

Boom! Boom! Boom!

"NO! STOP!"

A tremendous wave of energy grew inside her, as if she had a hurricane inside!

She took off with fury to peck the giant. She was ready to do anything...anything to help Sparky!

But then the giant roared:
"If you come any closer, I will drop him and you will never see him again!"

So River held herself back—she held her hurricane inside and didn't move a feather. The giant took Sparky away.

River secretly followed the giant to his castle. She saw that there were guards everywhere with big ears. So she waited quietly all night.

The next day, she flew around the castle and came to the window of the room where Sparky was being held. She didn't make a sound so the guards wouldn't hear her.

She desperately wanted to warn Sparky when she saw the giant coming, but she held her "squawk" in her throat.

She heard Sparky Tweet! Tweet!
The hurricane inside her grew again, ready to help Sparky—ready to do anything!

Boom! Boom! Boom!

...but she could not do anything...
She knew that doing anything would put Sparky in more danger. She held it all in and did not move.

Every evening, River would go to the window while making sure Sparky wouldn't see her.
She saw the giant scare Sparky.
She saw the giant hold Sparky's wings.
She saw the sparkle slowly fade from Sparky's eyes.

Boom! Boom! Boom!

Her heart kept pounding.
But she couldn't do anything. She held it in.
The hurricane inside her grew even bigger.

As Sparky got bigger, she wanted to tell him to open the lock and fly out. But she held her squawk inside because she knew the giant and the guards would hear her.

And she wasn't sure if Sparky could fly fast enough to escape the giant and the guards.

After many seasons of watching, her claws became very stiff from clenching them— unable to grab Sparky and take him away. Her back became stiff because she had to hold herself back and not move.
She was no longer fluid like a river.

But she kept watching and waiting.
She was waiting for the day Sparky would be big enough to open the cage and realize that he could fly to freedom.

And so she kept watching...
She watched the giant roar.
She watched Sparky freeze.
She watched the sparkle further dim in Sparky's eyes.

Her eyes got weaker, as it was very difficult for her to see what was happening to Sparky. The "squawks" she held in grew bigger and blocked her throat.

On some days, she could barely fly to the tree from where she watched Sparky.

Then one day, when the giant was out, she felt that Sparky was ready.
She flew to his window and let out a low tweet to encourage him to fly...

Then a few moments later, she saw Sparky fly out of the window.
"Sparky! You did it!"

The beginning

The River Series

Sparky Can Fly
Sparky's Mama
Tweets and Hurricanes
Feathers
Flex
Roots
The River

www.RiverSpeaks.com

www.ingramcontent.com/pod-product-compliance
Lightning Source LLC
Chambersburg PA
CBHW061121010526
44112CB00024B/2939